The
LEADERSHIP
SECRETS of

OZ

Strategies from great and powerful to flying monkeys – unleash some magic in your management

simple ▶ truths®
small books. BIG IMPACT.

simpletruths.com

BJ GALLAGHER
Foreword by Ken Blanchard

Internal illustrations courtesy of the Library of Congress; illustrations by W.W. Denslow. Additional illustrations used: page 1, BeauStocker/Shutterstock; page 4, arigato/Shutterstock; page 5, Kraphix/Shutterstock

Published by Simple Truths, an imprint of Sourcebooks, Inc.
P.O. Box 4410, Naperville, Illinois 60567-4410
(630) 961-3900
Fax: (630) 961-2168
www.sourcebooks.com

Printed and bound in China.
QL 10 9 8 7 6 5 4 3 2 1

CONTENTS

FOREWORD

THE *WIZARD* OF *OZ* HAS BEEN ONE OF MY FAVORITE stories since I was a boy. I've watched the movie at least twenty times with my kids and, years later, with my grandkids. I've read the book and enjoyed all things Oz—including the movie *The Wiz*, the fabulous Broadway musical *Wicked*, and more.

Like millions of people around the world, I marvel at the adventures of Dorothy and her companions.

I cheer their progress as they walk along the yellow brick road; I share their fear when they are confronted by the Wicked Witch of the West and her flying monkeys; and I delight in their discoveries of new lands, new creatures, and new people. I am not alone in my love for the original book as well as the 1939 movie. *The Wizard of Oz* is one of the best loved stories in the world with a message that touches people's hearts across cultures, across continents, and across generations.

But the tale of Dorothy, the Tin Woodsman, the Scarecrow, and the Cowardly Lion is not just an iconic children's book and family movie. It is also a parable about life and leadership—about being your best self. It is the story of four very different characters, each in the midst of developing their own unique potential. It is an ensemble cast, a quartet of seekers longing to fulfill their destinies—to build their brains and cultivate courage while still following their hearts.

I'm a Raving Fan© of BJ Gallagher—and when you read this book, you will be too. She has done a marvelous job of distilling the unique leadership lessons from this timeless tale. BJ believes that life and learning should be fun, engaging, and challenging. What could be more fun, engaging, and challenging than making your own journey to the Emerald City? I invite you to begin by turning the page of this wonderful book...and taking your first step on the yellow brick road of your life.

Ken Blanchard

Ken Blanchard, coauthor of *The New One Minute Manager®* and *Collaboration Begins with You*

There's
no place like
HOME...

HONEST assessment of your talents and skills

OPEN to new challenges and changes

MAKING the most of every opportunity

EXPRESSING your ideas, insights, and creativity

INTRODUCTION

"The beauty of metaphor is that
it conveys not just information—
but meaning."

—WARREN BENNIS, LEADERSHIP EXPERT

E VERY ONCE IN A GREAT WHILE, A METAPHORICAL
story comes along that captures the human
experience in such a perfect way that it becomes an
eternal classic. *The Wonderful Wizard of Oz* is just

such a story—it is the tale of Everyman and Everywoman. More than a billion people have read the book, shared across generations and across continents. First published in 1900, L. Frank Baum's timeless tale echoes the stuff of ancient myth—powerful, compelling, dramatic. It is the hero's journey with a lead character who leaves home in search of happiness in a better world; who travels hither and yon on a personal quest; and who ultimately comes full circle, arriving back home to discover that the treasure sought was right there all along.

In Baum's tale of Oz, our hero is not a solitary seeker but a band of seekers—all feeling something lacking in themselves, all yearning for what is missing from their lives. The Scarecrow is convinced his life would be different if only he had a brain; the Tin Woodman thinks his life would be so much better if only he had a heart; and the Cowardly Lion just knows he could fulfill his destiny to be king of the jungle if only he had courage. Can't we all identify with them? How often do we think our lives would be better...if only we had more intelligence, more love, more courage, more something?

Dorothy is on a quest too. She longs for "someplace where there isn't any trouble"—no mother figure (Auntie Em) who seemed too busy to listen to a girl's silly concerns, no mean old neighbor (Miss Gulch) to complain about a sweet little dog (Toto), and no problems or difficulties of any kind. Surely such a place must exist—somewhere over the rainbow, where life was serene and idyllic. Dorothy longs to live in paradise. Every hero's journey involves a search for some kind of paradise, nirvana, promised land, El Dorado, Atlantis, heaven— someplace where the streets are paved with gold (or yellow bricks), everyone gets along peaceably, and there is no want, no need.

The hero's journey is a quest for a peaceful place, but it is also a quest for inner peace. The hero's journey is ultimately a quest to find the self. It is a universal quest—one with which we can all identify.

The Oz story has four heroes—an ensemble cast questing together—each seeking something personal, something uniquely his or hers. And when they finally reach the wonderful Wizard of Oz, they each get something different—but they all get what they need.

And, as with all journeys, this one isn't as much about the

destination as it is about the journey itself. Dorothy and her companions travel the yellow brick road, encountering a multitude of hazards and obstacles along the way—challenges we can all identify with: flying monkeys of fear who can carry us away, wicked witches of jealousy and resentment, alluring detours of poppy fields that can easily sidetrack us from our goals, and militant soldiers standing in the way of our liberation from insecurity and self-doubt. These are metaphors for the threats and dangers we all face in traveling the yellow brick road of our own careers and lives.

But the journey isn't all peril and obstacles—there are also good witches and mentors to call on when we need assistance as well as Munchkin friends and fans to cheer us on our way. We are not alone on our journey—support and encouragement are available at every turn.

And what of the Wizard? Unlike what the four seekers hoped for and expected, the Wizard does not tap them on the head with some wizardly wand and turn them into something they aren't. No, his job is simply to reassure the foursome that they are not lacking anything. He helps them recognize their own true talents and abilities. The Wizard's job is to enable the seekers to see themselves more clearly. He reminds them how smart, talented, and courageous they already are.

And let us not forget the shoes—those magic slippers that take us wherever we want to go. They are the mythical equivalent of wings on our feet, transporting us into the future of our dreams. We all have magic slippers—traveling shoes that represent the power of belief, the power of affirming what we really want, the power of claiming our heart's desire.

The story of Dorothy, the Scarecrow, the Tin Woodman, and the Cowardly Lion—and Toto too—is the story of all who seek to become leaders in their own lives. It is the quest to discover your true self—to develop your own brains, heart, and courage—and to help others do the same.

PART I

Building *Brains*

"What would you do with a brain if you had one?"

—*Dorothy*

Brains Lesson #1

Leaders Practice Divergent Thinking and Look for Alternative Solutions to Problems.

Now look here, Dorothy, you ain't using your head about Miss Gulch. You'd think you didn't have any brains at all.

I have so got brains.

Well, why don't you use them? When you come home, don't go by Miss Gulch's place. Then Toto won't get in her garden, and you won't get in no trouble. See?

Oh, Hunk, you just won't listen, that's all.

Well, your head ain't made of straw, you know.

Human beings are capable of two kinds of thinking: convergent thinking and divergent thinking. *Convergent* thinking is the kind we use when there is only one right answer to a problem. Two plus two always equals four. There is only one right answer. When was the Declaration of Independence formally adopted? On July 4, 1776. That's the only right answer. What is your blood type? There is only one right answer. Convergent thinking is perfect for computing numbers, answering questions on history exams, and dealing with the basic facts of science, among other things.

Divergent thinking is the kind we use when there are several right answers (maybe even more than several) to a question or problem. Smart leaders know that most business problems—especially people problems—have more than one possible solution. The fact is there may be many good—even great—solutions to a problem. Being a smart leader means getting good at divergent thinking.

In the dialogue between Dorothy and the farmhand, Hunk, you can see that Hunk was using divergent thinking to help Dorothy solve her conflict with Miss Gulch. If Hunk and Dorothy had spent a little longer on the topic, they could have come up with even more solutions—like putting Toto on a leash to keep him from going into Miss Gulch's garden or leaving Toto at home altogether.

But Dorothy wasn't interested in finding a solution that would work for everyone—in this instance she was more interested in being right than looking for solutions. Dorothy was playing the victim, failing to look at her own behavior (and her dog's) and not owning up to how she participated in creating the problem. (Alas, even movie heroes and heroines aren't perfect! In them we can see our own human failings.)

In this scene from the Oz story, Hunk is stepping up to the role of leader, trying to teach young Dorothy how to use her brain—how to develop divergent thinking in order to solve problems. In Hunk we see how anyone and everyone can be a leader in life and at work. Leadership is not limited by position, job title, or status. Hired hand Hunk was setting a good example for the orphan Dorothy, who had not yet begun her own journey to becoming a leader.

BRAINY QUESTIONS AND ACTION TIPS

1. While divergent thinking is something we're all capable of, many of us have neglected this type of thinking due to our years of schooling—most of which emphasizes convergent thinking rather than creative divergent thinking. The good news is you can relearn it. Just like a muscle that has atrophied from disuse can be strengthened with exercise, your brain's divergent creativity can be strengthened with practice and mental exercise.

Read books on creativity; use puzzles to stimulate your brain's problem-solving ability; practice brainstorming work problems, especially in small groups where you can all develop your creative thinking together.

2. Practice divergent thinking first with small problems, ones that are neither urgent nor important. It takes time and practice to rebuild your brainpower. Don't expect to be Einstein right away. Take baby steps. Start small and build your brains over time.

3. Watch and learn from others who are already good at divergent thinking. Read about and study the lives of creative people like Benjamin Franklin, Thomas Edison, Steve Jobs, Madame Curie, Oprah Winfrey, Walt Disney. Look around your organization and see who's known for being an out-of-the-box thinker. Spend time with those people; learn from them; emulate them. If you want their brainpower, learn how to cultivate it in yourself.

Brains Lesson #2

Leaders Learn from Their Experiences, Especially Mistakes.

What have you learned, Dorothy?

Well, I—I think that it—it wasn't enough to just want to see Uncle Henry and Auntie Em—and it's that—if I ever go looking for my heart's desire again, I won't look any further than my own back yard. Because if it isn't there, I never really lost it to begin with! Is that right?

Dorothy learned many leadership lessons on her journey to Oz and back—and there is no way she could have learned them without leaving home. She had to go out into the world, searching for "somewhere over the rainbow," before she could gain new perspective and realize that she had what she needed all along—home was where her heart was.

Wouldn't it be wonderful if we could all see into the future and learn our lessons without experiencing the struggle, hard work, and pain firsthand? Yes, of course it would. But we can't. Experience is the best teacher. As Mark Twain wryly pointed out: "A man who carries a cat by the tail learns something he can learn no other way."

Talk to successful people, and they will tell you that they learned more from their failures and mistakes than they did from their triumphs. Thomas Edison is a shining example. When asked if he ever worried about failure, Edison said, "I have not failed. I've simply found 10,000 ways that won't work." Edison was one of the world's most creative inventors and business leaders: he invented the lightbulb, the phonograph, the stock ticker, a battery for an electric car, a mechanical vote recorder, and many useful telecommunications devices. Every "mistake" he made in the process taught him something about what worked and what didn't work. How else could he have learned what he needed to learn, except by experience?

1. What challenging experiences have you had that helped you develop as a leader? What did you learn about yourself? What leadership strengths did you discover or develop? What leadership weaknesses did you find in yourself? Can you think of leadership experiences you'd like to have in the future? What do you need most to learn?

2. How can you help others develop their own leadership skills? Are there ways you can involve them in projects that will challenge them? How can you contribute to a learning organization in which everyone can grow and develop his or her own latent leadership abilities?

3. You may not be able to get the experience you need if you stay on the farm in Kansas. Like Dorothy, you may have to journey to Oz, or your local equivalent, to become a more skillful leader. Are

there leadership experiences outside your organization that you could learn from? Can you get involved in a Rotary Club or other service organization? Can you contribute to the next generation of leaders by coaching a kids' soccer team or volunteering as a scout leader? Can you get leadership experience in your community, church, or synagogue? Can you get involved in local political groups and hone your leadership skills there?

ℬrains ℒesson #3

Leaders Know How and When to Speak... and When It's Wise to Keep Quiet.

 I haven't got a brain...only straw.

How can you talk if you haven't got a brain?

 I don't know... But some people without brains do an awful lot of talking...don't they?

Yes, I guess you're right.

Steel magnate Henry Kaiser used to say, "If your work speaks for itself, don't interrupt." He understood that actions speak louder than words and that people watch what you *do* more than they listen to what you *say*.

Kaiser also understood that talk is cheap—it's easy to spout off about all kinds of things, especially if you're in a leadership position and others feel compelled to listen to you. But if you don't know what you're talking about, you're better off staying silent or deferring to experts who do know what they're talking about.

Years ago, a young tax attorney named Bob Dedman worked for H. L. Hunt, one of the silver baron Hunt brothers. Hunt often introduced Dedman as "the smartest man in the room." Years later, I had the opportunity to interview Dedman, and I asked him if that was true—was he, indeed, the smartest man in the room?

Dedman replied: "Whenever I attended a meeting, I always sat quietly for a while and just listened to others voice their opinions. There were often some strong differences of opinion, as you can imagine among a bunch of high-powered business executives. If someone asked my opinion, I'd demure until I was ready to speak. I wanted first to make sure that I had listened carefully to everyone's point of view.

"When I finally spoke, I would offer a solution that contained elements of what everyone had said, enough so that they would feel their position was heard and acknowledged. I synthesized an option that everyone could agree with. It may not have been everything to everyone, but it was enough from everyone that they could all get on board. If that makes me the smartest man in the room, well then, yes, I guess I was."

Dedman smiled and winked, and I understood how Dedman had risen from tax attorney to becoming a hugely successful entrepreneur—owner of twenty-six country clubs, city clubs, and resorts across the country. By the end of his career, Dedman was known as "the richest man in golf."

BRAINY QUESTIONS AND ACTION TIPS

1. Are you a good listener? Do you know how to "read between the lines" to discern what's not being said as well as what is being said? Can you hear the message as well as the meta-message

(the feelings and ideas that are underlying the spoken words)? Can you read body language and facial expressions? Are you able to pick up the emotional tone of conversations and establish rapport with others? Are you skillful at active listening—quietly delving deeper into the multilayered messages others are communicating? If there is one skill that leaders at all levels need to master, it is the skill of effective listening.

2. My mother use to admonish: "God gave you two ears but only one mouth. Use them in that proportion." My father had his own favorite warning: "Make sure the brain is fully engaged before opening the mouth." I didn't realize it at the time, but they were both teaching me great lessons in leadership.

3. Sometimes the quietest people have the best insights into a situation or problem—precisely because they're quiet. While others are busy talking, complaining, speculating, opining, and/or showing off their verbal skills to impress the boss, quiet

people are listening, analyzing, thinking, evaluating, and gaining deeper under-standing. Seek out these quiet ones; ask them what they think; solicit their perspectives and opinions. Ask if they have suggestions. Create a safe space where they can offer their insights and ideas without being interrupted or overwhelmed by their more talkative peers. Pay attention to the quiet ones— you might be surprised at their wisdom.

Brains Lesson #4

Leaders Know That Learning Is Lifelong.
They Pursue Formal Education When They Need It.

 They have one thing you haven't got: a diploma. Therefore, by virtue of the authority vested in me by the *Universitartus Committiartum E Pluribus Unum*, I hereby confer upon you the honorary degree of ThD.

 ThD?

 That's...Doctor of Thinkology.

Many leaders get their education in the School of Hard Knocks, and most go on to get advanced degrees at the College of Painful Experience. Everything they learn is valuable, to be sure. But sometimes work experience and life experience aren't enough—sometimes it's essential to return to the classroom for some formal education and a certificate or diploma. Smart leaders know that there are times when what they need is a break from their on-the-job learning to spend time getting current on best practices in their industry or profession.

Putting yourself in a formal educational setting—whether it's at a university, professional school, or graduate program—can be invaluable not just for what you learn from the professors but for what you learn from your fellow participants. Comparing notes with others in your field can give you new ideas about how to handle your organization's tough challenges. Working on class projects together can help you discover new markets for old products and services as well as new products and services for old markets. Often, the learning that goes on between students is more powerful than the learning that goes on between students and professors.

Professional conferences offer many of the same benefits of

formal classroom experiences without the diploma or certificate. It doesn't matter so much whether you choose to continue your learning at a college, university, or professional conference—what matters is that you're always open to learning. In so doing, you're enhancing your own career prospects, your earning potential, and your organization's chances of success as well.

BRAINY QUESTIONS AND ACTION TIPS

1. When did you last spend some time in a classroom learning situation? When did you last attend a professional conference? What sorts of formal learning opportunities are available in your industry or profession? Are you availing yourself of what they have to offer?

2. How important are degrees and certification in your profession or business? Would further formal education help advance your career, or are you better off focusing on learning on the job?

Would it be a good idea to consult with your boss or mentor to ascertain if more formal education would be a good investment of your time and energy?

3. If you're a boss yourself, what kinds of formal development opportunities do you make available to your team? What do you offer in the way of support and encouragement to those who need further education? What's the payoff to your organization? What's the payoff to your employees?

Brains Lesson #5

Leaders Understand That Everyone Is Born with a Certain Mental Capacity and Level of Intelligence. There's No One to Thank, No One to Blame. It's What You Do with Your Mental Capacity That Counts.

The sum of the square roots of any two sides of an isosceles triangle is equal to the square root of the remaining side. Oh joy! Rapture! I got a brain! How can I ever thank you enough?

You can't.

Everyone is born with a brain. We each have a certain amount of IQ potential to develop as we grow into adulthood—not just a specific number but rather a range, determined largely by heredity

and early-life nutrition and nurturing. Scientists are learning more all the time about how far each of us can expand our IQ, but so far it appears that it's not infinite—there are upper limits beyond which our IQs cannot develop, no matter how much we study and learn.

But what is *unlimited* is the use to which you put your IQ, your innate intelligence. We can all think of famous people who didn't seem to have high IQs but went on to discover, invent, create, and develop phenomenally successful products, services, and businesses. The intellectual hand they were dealt at birth is not what made them rich, famous, and successful—it was how they played their hand that enabled them to rise above others with equal or greater intelligence. In other words, what you *do* with the IQ you've got is just as important as—or more important than—just your intelligence alone. As legendary screen star Sophia Loren pointed out, "…some people with mediocre talent, but with great inner drive, go so much further than people with vastly superior talent."

In the Oz tale, what was holding the Scarecrow back was not a lack of brains but a lack of belief in himself. He had all the brains he needed—he had as much brains as (or more than) other creatures. He just didn't understand that fact and, as a result, had been underestimating himself and probably underachieving until the Wizard pointed that out. Sometimes that's all we need—someone to hold up a mirror for us so we can see ourselves and our talent more clearly.

Brainy Questions and Action Tips

1. What are your natural talents, skills, and abilities? Make a list of what you think your strengths and capabilities are. Then share your list with a trusted friend, coworker, mentor, coach, or boss. Ask that person to review your list and see if there's anything you're not seeing in yourself. Perhaps you want to rank-order your skills and/or ask someone to do the same. Find out if you see yourself the way others see you.

2. Are you utilizing your natural intelligence, skills, and talents to maximum benefit? Do you have abilities that are lying dormant

within you, going unused or underused? Do you want to tap into some of these latent abilities and nurture them? What do you stand to gain by developing them? How might you enhance your job satisfaction—and career prospects—by doing so?

3. Are there ways you can help others develop their maximum potential? Can you encourage coworkers and colleagues to stretch and grow? If you're a team leader, how can you be a "wizard" for the people who report to you? How can you help them develop to their fullest potential? If everyone in your organization brought all their skills and talents to the table, how would this benefit your organization?

Brains Lesson #6:

Sometimes Even the Brainiest Leader Needs a Little Acknowledgment, Recognition, and Affirmation.

> Why, anybody can have a brain. That's a very mediocre commodity. Every pusillanimous creature that crawls on the Earth or slinks through slimy seas has a brain. Back where I come from, we have universities, seats of great learning, where men go to become great thinkers. And when they come out, they think deep thoughts and with no more brains than you have. But they have one thing you haven't got: a diploma.

Sometimes what people need may not be more formal education but, rather, recognition and acknowledgment of what they already know. Such was the case with the Scarecrow. He had ideas; he was creative and resourceful; he could see the forest as well as the trees; he was insightful and thoughtful. His problem was that he didn't know how much he knew.

The Scarecrow, like many other bright, talented, creative people, just needed a little acknowledgment. He needed someone—a respected authority figure—to recognize his savvy and smarts. He needed to see himself through others' eyes in order to honor his own intelligence.

It would be great if we didn't need validation from others in order to see our own genius, and there are plenty of people who don't: Bill Gates of Microsoft, Steve Jobs of Apple, Mark Zuckerberg of Facebook, athlete Tiger Woods, singer Lady Gaga, architect Frank Lloyd Wright, actor Tom Hanks, financial guru Suze Orman, and the brilliant Buckminster Fuller. None of them felt a need for a piece of paper to validate their intelligence—all are college dropouts.

Others, such as Daymond John of FUBU, music mogul Jay-Z, and actress Catherine Zeta-Jones, didn't drop out of college—they never attended college at all! They knew they didn't need a diploma to follow their dreams and achieve success.

That's not to say that a little validation and encouragement now and then isn't helpful. Of course it is. Whether in the form of a certificate or diploma, applause and public acclaim, or, best of all, financial success, we all like to receive some form of external validation that we're on the right track—that what we're doing is appreciated by others.

BRAINY QUESTIONS AND ACTION TIPS

1. What forms of validation mean the most to you? Do you gauge your talent, skill, and achievement by certificate, awards, and/or

diplomas? Are applause and fame meaningful to you? Does recognition from peers and colleagues mean the most to you? How do you assess your professional accomplishments and career success? Are you hungry for some form of validation that you haven't yet received?

2. Do you take time to validate others? Do you give positive feedback to your peers and coworkers? Do you compliment others on a job well done? If you supervise and manage others, how do you let them know how they're

doing? If you're not in the habit of acknowledging and recognizing the talent, skill, and contributions of others, it's never too late to start doing it.

3. "Feedback is the breakfast of champions," according to Ken Blanchard, leadership guru and coauthor of *The One Minute Manager.* "How am I doing?" is the question on everyone's mind. People want and need to know where they stand in terms of their boss's performance expectations. People also like to know where they stand in relation to others in their organization. Whether we like to admit it or not, we humans are acutely status conscious—much like other pack animals. We feel more comfortable and secure when we know where we stand in the pecking order. As the "alpha dog" in your pack, one of the important things people look to you for is clear, unambiguous, helpful feedback. If someone is doing a first-rate job, applaud that person and encourage him or her to keep up the great work. And if someone isn't performing well, let him or her know

tactfully but clearly, then redirect so he or she can improve. Let people know you have confidence that they can do better. As leader, you are the coach of your team, and winning coaches are in constant communication with their team members so everyone knows how they're doing.

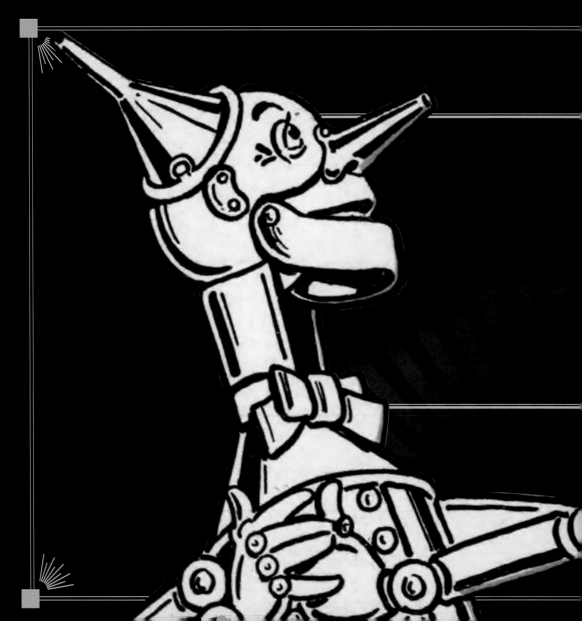

PART II

Heeding Your

Heart

"Back where I come from there are men who do nothing all day but good deeds. They are called phila...er, phila...er, yes, er, Good Deed Doers."

—*The Wizard of Oz*

Heart Lesson #1

Leaders Know Themselves. They're Clear about Who They Are—and Who They Aren't.

> Are you a good witch, or a bad witch?

> I'm not a witch at all. I'm Dorothy Gale from Kansas.

> Oh. Well, is that the witch?

> Who, Toto? Toto's my dog!

Effective leaders are clear-eyed and clear-headed. They are good about assessing the strengths and weaknesses of the people they lead, and they are even better at assessing their own strengths and weaknesses. That's one of the skills that enable them to rise to leadership positions. They have no illusions about themselves. They are wary of blind spots, and they solicit feedback from mentors, colleagues, and others to minimize any chance for self-deception. The more they know about themselves and the deeper their level of self-awareness, the less likely they are to get derailed in their careers.

Years ago, when I was a middle manager at a large metropolitan newspaper, I had a meeting with one of the senior executives. I was upset about something—though I can't remember now what it was—and feeling a little subdued and vulnerable. The executive noticed. "You should be like this more often," he said. "You're usually so pushy and abrasive."

"Really?" I asked. "Could you be more specific? Can you give me some examples of when I'm pushy and abrasive?" I genuinely wanted to understand what he was talking about because he was a powerful exec, and if he perceived me negatively, it certainly didn't bode well for my future with the company. Also, if he perceived me as pushy and abrasive, perhaps others did too. I needed to know more.

Our conversation went well because I didn't get defensive. I genuinely wanted to know what I was doing that made him view me in negative terms. I encouraged him to elaborate and then thanked him for the valuable coaching. "I want to be successful here, so I really appreciate you taking time to give me this feedback. You've given me much to think about. Thank you!"

After I left his office, I had plenty of time to reflect on what he said. I could check out his feedback with others whose opinions I respected. I could ask my colleagues if they saw me as pushy and abrasive. I could weigh and evaluate his comments to determine whether I needed to change. I learned something about myself from that conversation—and I learned something about him too. I learned that he did not like women who were confident and assertive. Their behavior was off-putting to him. He was an older man who preferred women with a softer, more feminine interpersonal style. That was very helpful to know so that I understood where he was coming from and knew to adjust my tone a bit whenever I had occasion to interact with him.

I thought about what he said, and I could see how my style might appear pushy and aggressive to him. I recognized that I probably needed to modulate my confidence and assertiveness in certain situations and with certain people—especially him. I don't have to be all-alpha, all the time. I can assess each situation and make subtle adjustments in my leadership repertoire in order to enhance my interpersonal effectiveness. The more I know about myself, the more I can play to my own strengths and minimize my weaknesses.

HEART-FULL QUESTIONS AND ACTION TIPS

1. Smart leaders welcome feedback from others—their bosses, their colleagues, and the people who work for them. They also seek feedback from customers and clients. They want it all—the good, the bad, and the ugly—because they know that they can't improve if the people they work with don't tell them the truth about how

they're perceived. There are a number of ways, both formal and informal, to solicit feedback from those you work with. One way is to utilize a 360-degree performance evaluation system instead of the old-fashioned and ineffective one-way performance review. With 360-degree systems, leaders receive structured feedback in written form from the people above them (bosses), people lateral to them (peers), and people below them (employees)—hence, 360-degree feedback. Of course, the system needs to be well-constructed, fair and balanced, and well-administered in order to achieve the desired result. If the system isn't well-designed or carefully managed, it will be ineffective and might even backfire.

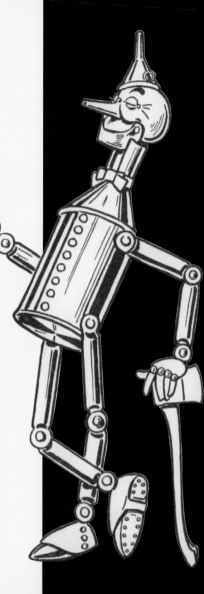

2. Smart leaders know how to make it safe for others to give them honest feedback. It's important that you cultivate trust and respect in your work relationships. Encourage feedback with questions like: "I respect you and value your perspective. Would you be willing to give me some feedback on how this project is going? How is the team doing? And how am I doing? Can you suggest ways that I might help my team be more effective?" And if someone gives you negative feedback or criticizes you, don't react with hurt feelings or anger. If people don't feel safe to give you honest feedback, you'll never know for sure how well you're doing as a leader.

3. Here's something to keep in mind: A complaint is a gift. When someone complains to you about your role as leader, treat the complaint as a valuable gift—because it is. If you're doing something that diminishes your leadership effectiveness and no one tells you about it, you can't fix it. You'll just go on shooting yourself in the foot and being less of a leader because of it. If someone gives you negative feedback, thank

the person. Ask him or her to tell you more. Ask for specific examples so you can better understand where you're falling short. And tell the person you appreciate the candid feedback because you want to be a better leader and you need information in order to do that. It's hard to welcome complaints as gifts—we are so conditioned to see complaints as something bad. But if you can retrain yourself to see feedback as friendly, all feedback—especially negative feedback—will help you grow as a leader.

Heart Lesson #2

Leaders Practice an Attitude of Gratitude. Rather Than Complain about What They Don't Like in a Situation, They Focus on What's Good about It.

 Oh, but anyway, Toto, we're home. Home! And this is my room, and you're all here. And I'm not gonna leave here ever, ever again, because I love you all, and—oh, Auntie Em—there's no place like home!

The human mind is a mismatch detector—it always notices what's wrong before it notices what's right. Everyone's mind is like that—your mind, my mind, and Dorothy's mind too.

It's not that we're all negative, fault-finding, unhappy people. It's just the way our minds work, probably because it serves our survival by alerting us to potential danger in our environment. Think about what life was like in the caveman days of early human history. When you came back to your cave after a day of hunting or gathering and noticed something amiss in your cave, it was a good indicator of an imminent threat. Being alert to something wrong helped ensure your survival. So the human brain evolved to always notice "something wrong" in any and all situations.

The problem is our brains have gotten so good at noticing what's wrong that we often overlook or ignore everything that's *right* in our situation. We don't see all the good stuff going on around us. We only notice the bad stuff, the things we don't like.

Dorothy is a perfect example. She had an aunt and uncle who loved her, she lived in a nice little farmhouse in the heartland of America, and she enjoyed the companionship of a devoted little dog. She had friends and family, she was in good health, and she had a good life. But she didn't think about those things. She didn't count her blessings because she didn't even notice those blessings.

Fortunately, we don't have to have our houses blown away to a strange land in order to appreciate all the good things in our lives. We don't have to lose everything in order to appreciate what we had. We need only change our thinking. We need only retrain our minds to focus on what's right rather than what's wrong in our job and workplace. We can choose what we pay attention to. We can learn to celebrate what's right with the world rather than complain about what's wrong.

HEART-FULL QUESTIONS AND ACTION TIPS

1. How well do you practice an attitude of gratitude? How often do you appreciate the many blessings in your life? Do you take time to acknowledge and enjoy them? An attitude of gratitude doesn't just happen automatically for most of us. Because our mind is a mismatch detector, we often find things to complain about—both at work and at home. It's easy to notice things we don't like about our boss, the people we work with, and our job. But complaining doesn't make us happy. It keeps us

stuck in unhappiness and discontent. One way to begin to retrain your mind—and to cultivate an attitude of gratitude—is to sit down and make a Gratitude List. Just get a sheet of paper or note card and make a list of all the things you like about your job, your boss, your coworkers, your organization. This may take a little time if you're not particularly happy in your current situation, but sit with it and be patient. Look for something—anything—to be grateful for and focus on that for now. It's a start.

2. It's easy to make the same mistake Dorothy made—to long for a better situation somewhere else, "over the rainbow," without noticing how good we have it right where we are. Most of us do it more often than we realize. We daydream about a better job, a better boss, a better organization, a better everything. To bring yourself back to the here and now—to create more happiness for yourself—try practicing Active Gratitude. Here's how: Make an appointment with yourself twice a day, for two or

three minutes every morning and every afternoon, and put it on your calendar. At the appointed time each day, stop what you're doing and look around to notice all the things you're grateful for. Walk about in your workspace and consciously notice things you like. Or get up and go get a cup of coffee or tea and along the way notice the people you like. Do this every day, twice a day, for twenty-one days and see if you don't feel happier about your work life.

3. Once you begin to practice Active Gratitude twice a day, start doing it more often. Next time you're in a meeting, take a look around to look for three things you're grateful for in that meeting. You don't have to do this out loud—just make mental notes to yourself. When you're commuting to work in the morning, think of three things you're grateful for about your workplace. When you're leaving work at the end of the day, think of three things you're grateful for that happened—or didn't happen—that day. If you're working on a really tough project, take a minute to reflect

on three things you're grateful for about that project. Continue to train yourself to look for aspects of your job and your organization that you're grateful for. Wise leaders—wise people—know that there is always something to be grateful for, no matter how tough the situation.

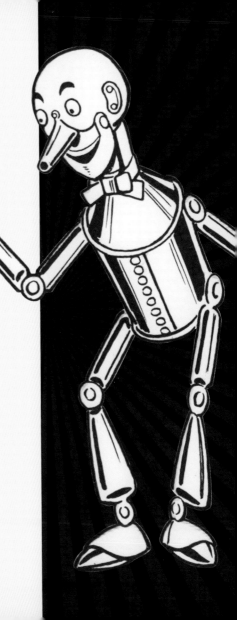

Heart Lesson #3

Leaders Know That Good Colleagues and Coworkers—Each with Unique Talents and Skills—Make a World of Difference in Achieving Success.

Oh, you're the best friends anybody ever had. And it's funny, but I feel as if I'd known you all the time, but I couldn't have, could I?

I don't see how. You weren't around when I was stuffed and sewn together, were you?

And I was standing over there, rusting for the longest time.

Still, I wish I could remember, but I guess it doesn't matter anyway. We know each other now, don't we?

Africans have a wise proverb: "If you want to travel fast, go alone. If you want to travel far, go with others." This is certainly true for leaders. If you want to lead successfully, you must get things done through others. You need to know the skills and talents of those you lead in order to play to their strengths. You must appreciate the diverse players on your team and leverage the creativity inherent in their diversity.

The full range of their skills and abilities may not be immediately apparent—it takes time to get to know the people on your team. And it's easy to make assumptions about others based on their appearance, age, ethnicity, gender, regional accent, personality, and occupation too. For instance, quiet introverts often get overlooked at work because extroverts love attention and know how to get it. Women often report that they, too, get overlooked, even when they speak up with a good idea. And people of color often feel frustrated at the stereotypes with which others view them.

We all make assumptions about others based solely on first impressions. As a leader, it's essential that you become aware of this tendency and always challenge yourself to look beyond the obvious.

HEART-FULL QUESTIONS AND ACTION TIPS

1. Are you aware of all the talents and skills of your team members? Most leaders aren't. They may know what a résumé says, and they may know what a job description says, but they don't really know all the skills their people have. As a result, many workers feel

underutilized. They'd like to contribute more on the job, but no one ever asks them to. Regular, frequent coaching sessions help ensure that leaders know what workers bring to the table. Talk to your people. Ask about their background, and experience, working in other places. Learn about skills and abilities they may have developed in the past. Technical skills, language skills, financial skills, organizational skills, people skills—you want to know as much as you can about the people you work with so you can tap into their experience.

2. One way to find out more about the people in your organization is to establish a formal skills inventory. Such an inventory provides a structured form that everyone fills out—listing the full range of their skills, talents, and abilities as well as experience and accomplishments. Most people have skills that they developed in previous jobs in other organizations—or skills that they developed off the job, say, in volunteer activities or church or community groups. A comprehensive skills inventory gives

leaders a way to find out about everyone's background so you know whom to turn to for special projects, planning, and/or problem-solving.

3. As a leader, do you feel like you should have all the answers to your organization's problems? Some leaders feel that their job is to "know it all." But wise leaders know that the people who are closest to the problem often have the best solutions. Ask for others' opinions about workplace issues. Listen attentively and respectfully. Follow up on good suggestions and ideas they offer. Reward their creative thinking, initiative, and problem-solving. As a leader, your job isn't to solve all the problems yourself but rather to enroll everyone in spotting and solving problems as well as preventing them when possible.

Heart Lesson #4

Leaders Know That There Is Strength in Vulnerability.

 As for you, my galvanized friend, you want a heart. You don't know how lucky you are not to have one. Hearts will never be practical until they can be made unbreakable.

But I still want one.

Sometimes the toughest leaders turn out to have the biggest hearts. Steve Jobs was the kind of guy with a reputation for being a tough, demanding, take-no-prisoners kind of boss.

I met Steve Jobs years ago when a Silicon Valley headhunter called me about a job opportunity at NeXT, the new computer company Jobs founded after he left Apple in the '80s. NeXT was

growing, and Jobs wanted to hire a director of executive development. Needless to say, I was intrigued and excited by the possibility of working with the living legend.

The interview process took many weeks. I made frequent trips to Redwood City to run the gauntlet of interviews with NeXT managers and executives, any one of whom could have vetoed me. Each time I passed muster, I proceeded to the next round of interviews. The lengthy selection process was a roller-coaster adventure, with more than the usual highs and lows of job interviewing. The process even included an audition: I was required to teach a management seminar for Jobs and his entire executive team (no pressure).

A couple weeks after the seminar, I was invited back for a final, one-on-one interview with Jobs. We talked about his vision for NeXT, his thoughts about leadership and building a successful company, his insights into his competitors. He asked me many questions, and I had a chance to ask him a few as well. Interested in getting the measure of the man, I included personal questions along with queries about the position and the company.

"How do you want to be remembered when you die?" I asked.

"I don't care if anybody remembers me," he said dismissively.

I wasn't expecting that answer. So after hesitating for a second, I tried a different tack. "OK, then, what do you want the people who love you to remember about you?"

Now it was Jobs's turn to hesitate. He thought for a couple seconds, then replied, "I want them to remember me as the best dad in the world."

Until then, I had admired and respected Steve Jobs...but now I loved him. I loved his humanity; I loved his commitment to his kids, present and future. And I loved his willingness to be open and intimate, if only for a brief moment. Like the Tin Man, Steve Jobs showed that he had a heart.

HEART-FULL QUESTIONS AND ACTION TIPS

1. As a leader, when do you feel it's appropriate to be vulnerable? Is it OK to show your emotions at work? Is it acceptable to

wear your heart on your sleeve about your work, your people, your organization?

2. Have you ever had your heart broken at work? Steve Jobs was fired from Apple, the company he had founded. You can bet that it broke his heart, big time. Have you ever been fired or laid off from a job or a company that you loved? How did your broken heart affect your career after that? Did getting your heart broken make you a better leader in the long run?

3. How do you help your followers when they get their hearts broken? Do you make it safe for them to be vulnerable at work? Can they share their fears and doubts as well as their dreams and aspirations? Is it OK to be human and vulnerable with you?

Heart Lesson #5

Leaders Know That Change Is a Normal Part of Everyone's Work Life and Career. We Don't Have to Like It, but We Do Have to Deal with It.

Goodbye, Tin Man. Oh, don't cry! You'll rust so dreadfully. Here's your oil can.

Now I know I've got a heart, 'cause it's breaking...

Goodbye, Lion. I know it isn't right, but I'm going to miss the way you used to holler for help before you found your courage.

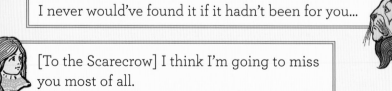
I never would've found it if it hadn't been for you...

[To the Scarecrow] I think I'm going to miss you most of all.

Being a change leader is a difficult job. Dorothy learned that as she led the way to Oz, picking up new followers along the way. She experienced confusion, fear, worry, and anxiety as well as excitement, joy, and the thrill of adventure as she and her group traveled the yellow brick road. They experienced many changes, especially within themselves. Journeys are like that—they change us.

History is full of stories of great change leaders. One of my favorites is Moses, who had an important job to do: liberating his people from Egypt and leading them to the Promised Land. It sounds simple, but it wasn't easy, for, as you'll recall, the Israelites didn't go straight from Egypt to the Promised Land. They wandered in the desert for forty years before arriving at their destination.

And what Moses didn't discover until well into his journey was that he actually had *two* jobs: to get the people out of Egypt...and to get Egypt out of the people (which was actually the harder of the two jobs). His people's traditional habits, old ways of thinking, assumptions, values, and culture all had to be transformed before they could establish a new culture in the Promised Land. An old generation literally had to die off in the desert while a new generation was born.

Many organizations—and perhaps yours is one of them—are wandering in the wilderness today. People are going through the predictable stages of organizational change while experiencing the normal feelings that accompany such change. There are five stages to the process: (1) denial; (2) upset, anger, betrayal, frustration, attempts to hold on to old, familiar ways; (3) acceptance, hitting bottom, giving up the old; (4) exploration and experimentation, tentatively moving forward into the unknown; and, finally, (5) new commitment, fully embracing a new reality, participating with creativity, vigor, and enthusiasm.

People going through change behave much like the Israelites did in the desert—complaining, criticizing their leaders, taking potshots at technology because it's a convenient target, creating false idols, and floundering around in confusion, anger, and resentment at the predicament in which they found themselves while wishing they could go back to good old days in Egypt because at least it was predictable, safe, and familiar (even if you did have to worship Pharaoh).

As a change leader, your first step in dealing with such enormous changes is to understand the process. Once you know the stages, it's at least a little bit reassuring to know that there is a beginning, middle, and end.

Second, understand that your own emotional reactions as well as those of your colleagues are normal. You would be weird if you didn't feel sadness, loss, grief, anger, confusion, and betrayal.

Third, extend compassion, patience, and understanding to those who are handling the change badly. Different people have varying capacities for going through the stages of change. Some move through the stages quickly with minimal pain, but many more suffer enormously. Some people get stuck at one stage or another and never make it to the fourth and fifth stages of change.

As a change leader, you bear a special responsibility to shepherd your people through the wilderness with skill, courage, vision, and all the leadership energy you can muster. You are the

Moses of your own team. Your job is to free your people from the old business paradigm and lead them to a Promised Land that no one can describe, much less point out on a map. Gird your loins, for your journey through the wilderness may very well last forty years or more. Be understanding and compassionate—your people are in pain, and they will criticize you, question you, berate you, and perhaps even revile you. Forgive them. Love them and care for them—they need good care and feeding on their arduous journey.

And, remember, Moses was a change leader—he didn't make it to the Promised Land himself. His job was to get his people there. So is yours.

HEART-FULL QUESTIONS AND ACTION TIPS

1. Many people have unrealistic expectations of their leaders—
    expecting them be Santa Claus, Superman, Daddy, and God all
    rolled into one. We expect change leaders to have the wisdom
    of Solomon, the soul of Gandhi, the strength of Hercules, the

compassion of Mother Teresa, and the enlightenment of Buddha. And heaven help these leaders if they turn out to be mere mortals—albeit smart, talented, good-hearted mortals. Hell hath no fury like disappointed followers. Moses had the same problem. When he wasn't able to transport his people to the Promised Land fast enough, they turned on him. "You're a terrible leader," they said. "We've been wandering in this desert for years, and the Promised Land is nowhere in sight," they complained. "You don't know where you're going." "We should go back to Egypt," some proposed. "At least with Pharaoh we knew what to expect." They lost their faith and built a golden calf to worship instead. What can you do as a change leader to manage your followers' expectations?

2. As part of his leadership duties, Moses was given the Ten Commandments to share with his people. *You* need your own personal set of commandments, too—the commandments of a change leader:

- People are illogical, unreasonable, and self-centered.

  Love them anyway.

- If you do good, people will accuse you of selfish ulterior motives.

  Do good anyway.

- If you are successful, you will win false friends and true enemies.

  Succeed anyway.

- The good you do today will be forgotten tomorrow.

  Do good anyway.

- Honesty and frankness make you vulnerable.

  Be honest and frank anyway.

- The biggest men and women with the biggest ideas can be shot down by the smallest men and women with the smallest minds.

  Think big anyway.

- People favor underdogs but follow only top dogs.

  Fight for a few underdogs anyway.

- What you spend years building may be destroyed overnight.

  Build anyway.

- People really need help but may attack you if you do help them.

  Help people anyway.

- Give the world the best you have, and you'll get kicked in the teeth.

  Give the world the best you have anyway.

3. Being a change leader can be a thankless job. You pour your heart and soul into creating a better future for your people, and

what do they do? Whine and complain. It's like driving cross-country with a backseat full of immature, impatient children who keep asking, "Are we there yet?" They have no understanding of the time it takes to get from one place to another. And just as children act out and make life miserable for the adult driving the car, so too do cranky, demanding, whining followers make life miserable for their change leader. The followers have no patience, no perspective, and no appreciation for all that their leader is doing for them. What can you do to take care of yourself in the absence of appreciation from your followers? Is there anyone you can turn to for encouragement and support?

These "Paradoxical Commandments" were written in 1968 by Kent Keith as part of a handbook for student leaders. And they're as relevant today as they were fifty years ago. Whether you're leading college students, corporate employees, nonprofit groups, professional associations, government agencies, or any other team, group, or organization, these commandments will stand you in good stead.

Heart Lesson #6

Leaders Know That at the End of the Day, What Counts Is Not Just the Dollars You Make— It's the Difference You Make.

A heart is not judged by how much you love; but by how much you are loved by others.

Think of the leaders who are much admired in the world today: Albert Einstein, Mother Teresa, the Dalai Lama, Steve Jobs, Warren Buffett, Gandhi, Abraham Lincoln, Golda Meir, Albert Schweitzer, Rosa Parks, Mozart, Gloria Steinem, William F. Buckley, Michelangelo, Franklin D. Roosevelt, Martin Luther King Jr., John F. Kennedy, Bill Gates, the Buddha, Madame Curie, Eleanor Roosevelt, Jesus, Florence Nightingale, Mohammed, Thomas Edison, George Washington, among others. What is it that we admire about them?

Their money? Their talent and skill? Their fame? Their successes in their fields? Yes, all that, to be sure. But in most cases it's something bigger that we admire—it's the difference they made in the world.

These leaders are admired, respected, and, yes, even loved by millions of followers and fans. These leaders continue to exert their influence across cultures, across continents, and across generations because the difference they made was so powerful, so profound, so transformative.

Not every leader makes a difference on a global level—most leaders don't. But every leader makes a huge difference to his or her followers. Even if you lead only a handful of people, you can make a very big difference to those people.

I am reminded of a well-known story:

One morning a man was walking down the beach. There had been a big storm the night before, and thousands of starfish had been washed up on the beach. In the distance, the man saw a little boy coming in his direction. As the two drew closer, the man could see that the youngster was picking up starfish and tossing them back into the water. When they got close enough to have a conversation, the man asked, "What are you doing?" The boy said, "I'm throwing these starfish back in the water so they don't die." The man shook his head and said, "You're just one little boy, and there are thousands of starfish here. How can you possibly hope to make any difference?" The boy thought about it a moment, then picked up another starfish and flung it into the surf. He turned to the man and said, "Well, I made a difference to that one."

As a leader, you, too, make a difference to the people around you. You make a difference just as that little boy did…one person at a time.

HEART-FULL QUESTIONS AND ACTION TIPS

1. What kind of a difference do you make to the people around you? Some leaders make a positive difference, while others make a negative difference. You can inspire people to achieve

their best—or you can belittle and criticize them with chronic fault-finding. You can motivate them with encouragement and praise—or you can motivate them with fear and intimidation. You have the power to make their work lives wonderful—or terrible. What difference are you making to others?

2. Every leader makes a difference—sometimes a huge difference, sometimes a more modest difference. But every difference counts. What kind of difference do you want to make?

3. Can you think of leaders who have made a difference in your life? Who were they? What did they do that had such a positive effect on you? What did you learn from them? How did they change your career and/or your life?

PART III

Cultivating *Courage*

"Frightened? Child, you're talking to a man who's laughed in the face of death, sneered at doom, and chuckled at catastrophe... I was petrified."

—*The Wizard of Oz*

Courage Lesson #1

Courage Doesn't Mean Having No Fear. Courage Means Feeling Fear and Taking Action Anyway.

 Your Majesty, if you were king, you wouldn't be afraid of anything?

Not nobody! Not nohow!

 Not even a rhinoceros?

Imposerous!

 How about a hippopotamus?

Why, I'd thrash him from top to bottomus!

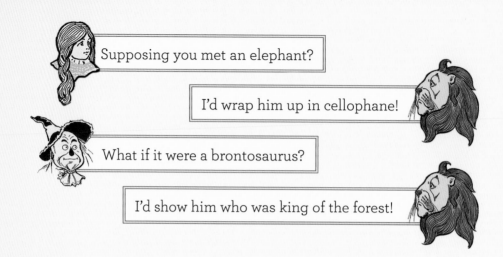

Fear is one of the major themes in the Oz story. Dorothy is afraid of Miss Gulch; she squeals in fear when she falls into the pigpen; she is terrified as the tornado approaches. She's afraid that Auntie Em is ill and dying, so she must hurry home. She's afraid when a witch appears, as she's never seen a witch before. She's afraid of the flying monkeys. So it's clear that Dorothy is not someone who never feels fear—rather, she feels her fear and takes action anyway.

We see this theme again and again throughout the Oz

story—with all the lead characters. The Scarecrow, the Tin Woodman, and, of course, the Cowardly Lion all experience fear many times on their journey to Oz, but they don't let fear stop them. They feel the fear and keep going anyway.

Fear is a fact of life. Everyone feels it many times in the course of their lives. Leaders feel fear, as do their followers. Fear is a normal, universal, human emotion.

Leaders know how to turn fear into fuel. Leaders channel their fear into constructive action. They feel the adrenaline that fear releases in their bodies, and they use it to propel themselves forward. Both the Wizard and Dorothy knew this, as evidenced in the quote above.

Fear can be a great motivator when it's a healthy fear, a legitimate fear. Great performers often say that the butterflies in their stomach before a performance actually energize them to rise to the occasion. They credit their stage fright with helping them to become stars by stimulating them to do their very best. Nervousness is energy, and energy can be harnessed and used to achieve positive results.

Courageous Questions and Action Tips

1. Think about a time when you felt fear and took action in spite of your fear. What was it that enabled you to rise above your fear? Is it something you can teach others how to do? How can you help your colleagues and/or employees handle their own fears?

2. What have you learned from observing other people move through fear and rise to the occasion? Are there role models and examples of such behavior in your organization? What have you learned from them? Can you enlist them in teaching others how to do the same?

3. Recognize and reward people who demonstrate courageous behavior in the face of fear. Watch for people who are doing a great job handling their fears and who can be a good influence on others. Applaud them. Celebrate their courage. What you reward in your organization is what you'll get more of!

Courage Lesson #2

Courageous Leaders Have the Ability to Discern between Real Dangers and Imaginary Ones.

 Witch? Hmph, I'm not afraid of a witch. I'm not afraid of anything—except a lighted match.

I don't blame you for that.

Fear can be your friend or your enemy. There is a difference between healthy, sensible fear that keeps you safe and unhealthy, irrational fear that keeps you from taking action when you should.

The Scarecrow knew that fire was dangerous and something

to be avoided at all costs. He also knew that a witch was something he could handle...unless, of course, she was a flame-throwing witch!

Courage, in tandem with experience and wisdom, enables a leader to discern between real dangers and imaginary ones. A courageous leader is not spooked by irrational fears of events that have a very low probability of ever happening. And a courageous leader has healthy respect for legitimate threats and takes due precautions to prevent and/or handle such threats.

COURAGEOUS QUESTIONS AND ACTION TIPS

1. To distinguish between real threats and illusory threats, it is often helpful to consult with trusted colleagues and coworkers. Check out your perceptions by sharing them with confidantes and allies. Ask for their feedback. Ascertain if they recognize the same threats you do.

2. Organizational threats can be internal as well as external, so make sure you are aware of what's going on inside your company or business as well as what's going on in the world around you. External threats can include marketplace dynamics, shifting demographics, changing technology, customer preferences, political climate, regulatory issues, media trends, and more. Internal threats might include gossip and rumors, morale problems, cash-flow problems, poor selection and hiring practices, inadequate training, racial tension, and gender issues, among others. Take time to do a periodic threat assessment with your team.

3. A courageous leader tells people the truth about what's going on. He or she knows that in the absence of real information, employees will make up their own—and their speculation and worries are always far worse than the truth! Rampant rumors and fear can paralyze an organization as well as cause some of your most valuable employees to start looking for work elsewhere. Counter fear with the truth. People can handle the truth. What they can't handle is not knowing what's really going on. A courageous leader treats people as adults—giving them all the information they need to help them to distinguish between legitimate fears and false ones.

Courage Lesson #3

Leaders Know That Courage and Wisdom Are Not the Same. Wisdom Means Knowing Which Battle to Fight; Courage Means Fighting the Battle You've Chosen.

 You, my friend, are a victim of disorganized thinking. You are under the unfortunate impression that just because you run away you have no courage; you're confusing courage with wisdom.

A wise leader picks and chooses battles. A courageous leader stands and fights the battles worth fighting. The Wizard is pointing out a very important distinction to the Cowardly Lion who doesn't realize that it is wise—and, yes, even courageous—to run from a battle that is not worth fighting. One has to weigh costs and benefits of each battle—whether it be an internal political battle, a competitive corporate battle, or a battle on the front lines of creativity and innovation. Sometimes the smart thing is to cut your losses and retreat, while other times the smart thing is to stand and defend your turf. There are no hard-and-fast rules to tell you when to do which. Such decisions must be made on a case-by-case basis.

Wisdom comes from experience, and the more experience one has, hopefully the wiser one is. But this isn't always the case—as with the Cowardly Lion, who had plenty of experience in running away but had never reflected on his experience long enough to glean wisdom from it. The Wizard had to help him see the wisdom in his responses to past encounters with danger.

How do you decide which battles are worth fighting and which to walk (or run) away from? There isn't a one-size-fits-all answer to this question, but you can break down the elements you need to consider in evaluating each situation:

- How important is this issue to me and my career?
- How important is it to my organization?

- What will it cost me to take on this issue? What do I stand to gain by getting involved?

- What will it cost my organization for me to engage in this problem? What does my organization stand to gain from my involvement?

- If I take it on and fail, what are the consequences for me, my team, my boss, my organization?

COURAGEOUS QUESTIONS AND ACTION TIPS

1. Know yourself. Are you the type of person who loves to tilt at windmills? Do you enjoy engaging in office politics and/or organizational debate and drama? If so, be careful that you don't involve yourself in so many battles that you wear yourself out with battle fatigue. Also, be careful that you don't become seen as a chronic troublemaker or fault-finder. Exercise caution. Seek advice and counsel from level-headed people you trust.

2. Be a good role model for others. If you have people who report to you, coach them on the criteria for distinguishing between an important issue worth taking a stand on and an issue that is only of passing importance and not worth extending time and energy on.

3. Wisdom entails the ability to learn from others' experiences as well as your own. You don't have to reinvent the wheel. Pay attention to others' experiences and learn from them.

Courage Lesson #4

Courageous Leaders Ask Others for Candid Advice to Ensure Their Decisions Are Smart and Doable. They Don't Surround Themselves with "Yes Men."

 All right, I'll go in there for Dorothy. Wicked Witch or no Wicked Witch, guards or no guards, I'll tear them apart. I may not come out alive, but I'm going in there. There's only one thing I want you fellows to do.

 What's that?

 Talk me out of it!

Sometimes a decision or action may seem courageous in the moment—particularly moments of high stress and urgency—but appearances can be deceiving. Courageous leaders are willing to take necessary action to save the day but are also willing to solicit input from trusted advisors to make sure they are not about to do something they'll regret later.

"Two heads are better than one," my mother used to say. And as usual, Mom was right. Those who are leaders—or who aspire to leadership—must be willing to seek others' opinions and perspectives before making an important decision. Going it alone, without soliciting input from others, can lead to disaster.

Strong leaders are courageous enough to handle differences of opinion. In fact, smart leaders actively seek out diverse perspectives in order to test their own thinking. We all have blind spots, and it can be very helpful to solicit feedback from people who are likely to disagree and have a different take on the situation. As leadership expert Warren H. Schmidt often said, "If six people in a room agree, five of them aren't thinking."

But it takes courage to listen to others tell you you're mistaken, you're wrong, and you're headed in the wrong direction. Leaders with fragile egos or who are insecure are unlikely to have the courage it takes to consider alternative points of view with a truly open mind. History is replete with disastrous outcomes caused by leaders who insisted "it's my way or the highway" and refused to consider the opinions and insight of those who saw things differently.

Leaders with courage understand that disagreement doesn't mean disloyalty. In fact, just the opposite! If someone in your organization voices a genuine difference of opinion, that person is demonstrating both loyalty and courage, for it seldom endears you to people to disagree with them. Such a person should be acknowledged and recognized as a valuable contributor. You may not agree—and you may decide to go ahead with your plans anyway—but that person gave you an honest opinion and, in so doing, gave you a valuable gift. Thank such people. Praise them. Reward them.

COURAGEOUS QUESTIONS AND ACTION TIPS

1. Make it safe for people to disagree with you. Don't shoot the messenger when someone presents information that doesn't

support your position. Don't punish those who see things differently. Instead, ask yourself, "How can I encourage everyone in my organization to share their best ideas and perspectives with one another?" If you want people to contribute their best thinking, you must demonstrate the courage of open-mindedness. You must be willing to be wrong and admit it.

2. When you have a different idea or perspective, pick the right time and place to express it. A good general rule of thumb is: "Praise in public and criticize in private." If you want to voice your agreement with someone's decision or action, do so publicly. A little praise goes a long way when it's done in front of others. But if you disagree with someone's decision or action, it's a good idea to do so privately, in a one-on-one situation, so as not to be seen as trying to embarrass or challenge that person's authority or expertise. Of course, if you're in a staff meeting or brainstorming session where ideas are being discussed and debated, then voicing a difference of opinion

is just fine. Let your common sense guide you as to where and when to offer an alternative perspective.

3. Do your homework and encourage others to do the same. Opinions are just opinions unless they are backed up with data and/or experience. Opinions are a dime a dozen and not worth much unless they're grounded in facts. To paraphrase an old cliché about teams: "Your group is only as strong as its weakest think." Set a good example by backing up your own opinions with solid data; encourage and acknowledge others when they do it too.

Courage Lesson #5

Leaders Show Courage When They Step In and Stand Up for Those Who Cannot Defend Themselves.

 I'll get you anyway, Pee-wee. [Chases Toto]

Shame on you! [Dorothy hits the lion on the nose]

[Sobbing] Why did you do that for? I didn't bite him.

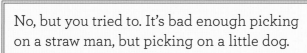 No, but you tried to. It's bad enough picking on a straw man, but picking on a little dog.

 Well, you didn't have to go and hit me! Is my nose bleeding?

Of course not.

Leaders with true courage do not bully or harass, nor do they tolerate others doing so. Effective leaders show respect and consideration for everyone in their organization, down to those in the lowliest positions. Everyone, no matter what pay grade or status, has an important contribution to make to the collective success and, as such, is worthy of respect and kindness.

A leader who bullies or intimidates is not a courageous leader—he or she is a coward. Whether a Cowardly Lion (as in the previous quote from the Oz story) or a Cowardly Corporate Leader, he or she is not the type of leader that anyone wants to follow. We pity such a leader and see the person for what he or she really is—a wimp.

Bullying and harassment are serious threats to the health and vitality of an organization. Workers who are ducking and dodging a bullying boss cannot possibly contribute their full talent, skill, and commitment. Those who feel they have to work in a fearful mode are distracted by having to constantly cover their posteriors.

A courageous leader stands up to bullies not only for their

own sake but for the sake of those who cannot defend themselves. A courageous leader is a champion for those who are too easily ignored, neglected, overlooked, or maligned in their organization. As in the example above, Dorothy stood up for the little dog that could not defend itself against a menacing lion. She demonstrated courage in the face of danger, and she put the lion on notice that such bullying would not be tolerated. In so doing, Dorothy established herself as a true leader, one worthy of respect—and she set an example for the other members of her team. She did so not just because she loved her little dog, Toto, but also because it was simply the right thing to do. You can be certain that she would have done the same thing even if the dog had not been hers.

COURAGEOUS QUESTIONS AND ACTION TIPS

1. Are there people in your organization who are in need of a champion? Are there individuals or groups of workers who feel intimidated or bullied by those in power? What can you do to

help them? What steps can you take to ensure that everyone in your organization feels like a valued member of the team and is treated with respect and consideration?

2. Certain forms of harassment and bullying are particularly egregious, like sexual or racial harassment. Do you have policies and procedures in place to protect everyone from such damaging, illegal, and immoral mistreatment? Are there resources available so that someone victimized by a bully can seek redress? Does your organization have a zero-tolerance policy against all forms of harassment and intimidation? What can you do to help protect your business from potentially expensive litigation?

3. If you witness someone being bullied or harassed, do you have the courage to step in and stop the abuse? What does it cost you to intervene? What does it cost you to *not* intervene?

Courage Lesson #6

Courageous Leaders Do the Right Thing.

> You cursed brat! Look what you've done! I'm melting! Melting! Oh, what a world! What a world! Who would have thought a good little girl like you could destroy my beautiful wickedness? Oooooh, look out! I'm going! Oooooh! Ooooooh!

Leadership expert Warren Bennis is often quoted as saying, "Managers do things right. Leaders do the right thing." Managers do things by the book. Leaders know when to throw the book out the window and do what's right, even if it isn't spelled out in the company policy and procedure manual.

Doing the right thing with customers might mean going the extra mile to make things right rather than say, "Sorry, it's not our

policy to do that." Doing the right thing can mean speaking truth to power if you think your organization is heading down the wrong path. Doing the right thing can involve stepping in to help resolve a conflict between colleagues or coworkers, even when you know it won't make you popular. Doing the right thing includes making tough decisions that will cause pain in the short run but make your organization stronger in the long run. It takes courage to do the right thing.

But doing the right thing does not mean ignoring all policies, procedures, and rules. Doing the right thing means knowing when to stick with regular protocol and when to do something different and better. It takes experience, wisdom, insight, and perspective—as well as courage—to do the right thing.

In the Oz story, Dorothy did the right thing in throwing water on the Wicked Witch of the West, though it was never her intent to kill. Dorothy was simply trying to put out the fire on the Scarecrow's arm—a fire started by the menacing witch. Dorothy knew that her friend was in mortal danger, so she didn't think twice. She simply

grabbed a nearby cleaning bucket filled with water and doused the Scarecrow's flaming arm. And, in the process, water splashed on the witch, causing her to melt away. That's the way it is with courage sometimes—you do the right thing to solve a problem, and in the process you actually solve a bigger problem. Sometimes acts of courage have unintended positive consequences that are more powerful than we could have anticipated when we took action.

Leaders foster courage in others first and foremost by being courageous themselves. They act on their convictions. When something is wrong, they step up and fix it. Courageous leaders don't wait for others to act.

They don't say, "That's not my job." Courageous leaders take initiative, and by doing so, they give their followers permission to do the same. Courage lives in action—not in fantasies and daydreams. Courage is as courage does.

COURAGEOUS QUESTIONS AND ACTION TIPS

1. Look around at your work situation. Is there an issue or a problem that needs addressing—something that perhaps you've been avoiding or procrastinating on because you dread dealing with it? What step(s) could you take today that would get you started on a solution? It doesn't have to be a big step—sometimes small steps lead to big results.

2. How can you support others in developing courage on the job? Do they refrain from courageous actions for fear of getting in trouble? Have they been conditioned to wait and look to others to take the lead? How can you create a courageous work

environment for everyone? What concrete steps can you take to reward courage when you see it in others? As Ken Blanchard often says, "Catch people doing something right...and reward them for it!"

3. Do you know when to do things right versus when to do the right thing? Under what circumstances to act in manager mode and go by the book and when is it appropriate to go beyond the book in order to do the right thing? How do you develop this type of insight and judgment within yourself? How can you help develop this important kind of discernment in others?

CONCLUSION

Wise Words from the Wizard of Oz

10 Wise Words

Read what my medal says: "Courage." Ain't it the truth?

9 Wise Words

I'm not afraid of anything—except a lighted match.

8 Wise Words

Oh, you're the best friends anyone ever had!

7 Wise Words

How can I ever thank you enough?

6 Wise Words

Be a lion, not a mouse.

5 Wise Words

There's no place like home.

4 Wise Words

I got a brain!

3 Wise Words

What a world!

2 Wise Words

Free Dorothy!

1 Wise Word

Home.

ABOUT THE AUTHOR

BJ Gallagher is a workplace expert, prolific author, and popular speaker. She writes business books that educate and empower, women's books that enlighten and entertain, and gift books that inspire and inform. Whether her audience is corporate executives, working women, or job seekers, her message is "The Power of Positive DOING." She motivates and teaches with empathy, understanding, and more than a little humor.

BJ's international business bestseller, *A Peacock in the Land of Penguins* (Berrett-Koehler), was endorsed by Archbishop Tutu and has sold more than 375,000 copies in twenty-three languages. Her previous business books include *Being Buddha at Work: 108 Ancient Truths on Change, Stress, Money, and Success* (Berrett-Koehler) with a foreword by the Dalai Lama, and *YES Lives in the Land of NO: A Tale of Triumph Over Negativity* (Berrett-Koehler), now published in ten languages.

BJ is a regular *Huffington Post* contributor. She has been featured on *CBS Evening News, The Today Show* with Matt Lauer, Fox News, PBS, CNN, and other television and radio programs. She is quoted frequently in various newspapers, women's magazines, and websites, including O *the Oprah Magazine, Redbook, Woman's World,* the *New York Times,* the *Chicago Tribune,* the *Wall Street Journal,* the *Christian Science Monitor,* the *Orlando Sentinel,* the *Financial Times* (UK), the *Guardian* (UK), MSNBC.com, CareerBuilder.com, CNN.com, and Forbes.com, among others.

In addition to writing books, BJ also conducts seminars and delivers keynotes at conferences and professional meetings across the country. Her corporate clients include IBM, Chevron, the U.S. Department of Veteran's Affairs, John Deere Credit Canada, Volkswagen, Farm Credit Services of America, the U.S. Department of the Interior, Phoenix Newspapers Inc., the American Press Institute, Infiniti, Nissan, and the *Atlanta Journal Constitution*, among others.

You can reach her at www.peacockproductions.com.

CHANGE STARTS WITH **SOMETHING SIMPLE.**

Pick from hundreds of titles at:
SimpleTruths.com

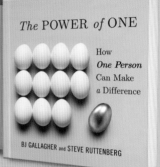

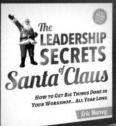

▷ Shop for books on themes like: teamwork, success, leadership, customer service, motivation, and more.

Call us toll-free at **1-800-900-3427**

A Teacher's Night Before Christmas

A Teacher's Night Before Christmas

Sue Carabine

Illustrations by Kathy Mitchell

GIBBS SMITH
TO ENRICH AND INSPIRE HUMANKIND

First Edition
14 13 12 11 10   5 4 3 2

Text © 1996, 2010 by Gibbs Smith
Illustrations © 2010 Kathy Mitchell

Published by
Gibbs Smith
P.O. Box 667
Layton, Utah 84041

1.800.835.4993 orders
www.gibbs-smith.com

Design by Renee Bond
Printed and bound in China
Gibbs Smith books are printed on either recycled, 100% post-
consumer waste, FSC-certified papers or on paper produced from a
100% certified sustainable forest/controlled wood source.

ISBN 13: 978-1-4236-1695-5
ISBN 10: 1-4236-1695-2

'Twas the night before Christmas,
    when at the North Pole,
St. Nicholas was ready
    to perform his great role.

His outfit was striking,
    all clean and well pressed,
from the fur on his hat
    to the trim on his vest.

Dasher and Dancer
  and the rest of the crew
were getting so restless
  awaiting their cue.

The bells on their reins
  just shimmered and glowed;
their coats shone with luster,
  as they strained at the load.

"I think we're all ready,"
  a deep voice announced,
then Santa jumped into
  the sleigh with a bounce.

"The list, fetch the list,
       my cheery young elf,
I need to count toys
       and make sure of myself."

The elf stared at Santa,
       his face looked quite blank.
"The list," he said softly,
       and his heart about sank.

"Why, you have it already,
       I'm sure that you do.
Look there in your sack,
       it's just hidden from view.

"Ho, ho, ho," said St. Nick.
       "This is not time for tricks.
I must get a move on
       or we'll be in a fix.

"A new list my computer
   can readily print.
Run along, little elf, or better yet, sprint."

The elf stood there trembling,
   his hopes all but dashed,
As he gently told Santa
   the hard drive had crashed.

"**N**o, no, no!" boomed out St. Nick.
"That list was checked twice.
It must print or we won't know
who's been naughty or nice."

Mrs. Claus stood there smiling
and patting young Prancer,
"Calm down my dear husband,
'cause I have the answer.

"Those wonderful people
who mold the world's future
can solve any problems—
I believe they're called 'Teacher.'

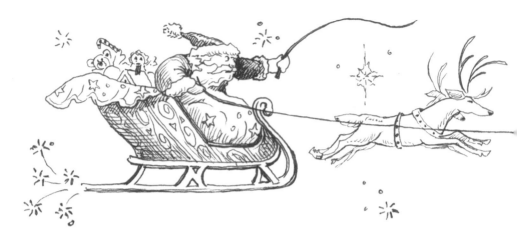

"I'll get the word to them
　　　from East Coast to West.
They've seen all the kids
　　　at their worst and their best.

"Just visit the teachers
　　　before you proceed
to the homes of the children
　　　who expect you this eve."

So Santa Claus, chuckling,
    sped on his way,
breaking all records
      while guiding the sleigh.

To the first teacher's home
      he went with great haste,
and she told him these secrets
      with no time to waste.

Mrs. Giles in third grade
      almost started to yell
when relating to Santa
      of Tom's Show & Tell.

He'd brought a small box
      with a wrapper beneath,
which, when he uncovered,
      showed Grandma's false teeth!

"**B**ut that was fine, St. Nick,"
she said with a smile,
"the children stopped giggling
after a while.

"And Tom is a good boy;
he does well on his tests.
Please make sure you leave him
the gifts he requests."

So the Jolly Old Elf
went fast on his way,
learning of kids from
what teachers would say.

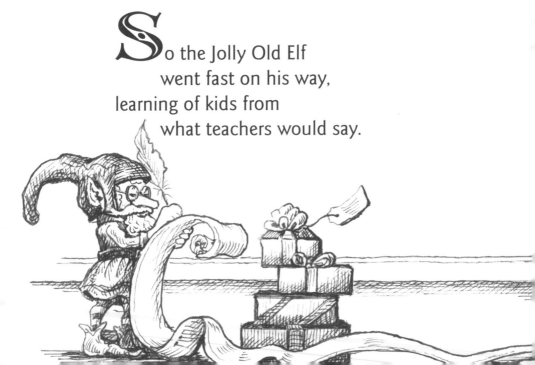

He came to a village
    that sparkled with snow,
where the faces of children
    in sleep had a glow.

Mrs. Jeffers was waiting to tell him of Jane,
who was there when it happened
    but wasn't to blame.

The plug just blew up,
    made a hole in the wall.
No one was hurt, not Jane's fault at all.

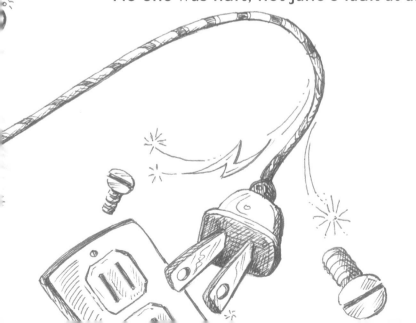

She has always loved science
and told her instructor
that from Santa she wanted
a super conductor.

"So please grant her wish,
for in you she believes,
and a Nobel Prize someday
she just might receive."

Santa laughed loudly
and nodded his head,
trying to remember
all that was said.

He enjoyed spending time
with these teachers so dear;
the love that they had
for their kids was quite clear.

The next town he came to
was filled with such light,
he just couldn't wait
to fill stockings that night.

But first St. Nick knew of
a teacher he'd meet
who would give him some facts
till his list was complete.

This time a twinkle
   appeared in the eye
of the teacher who told him
   who made the girls cry.

At five years of age,
   Billy never would miss

any chance that he had
   to give each girl a kiss!

"But, my dear Santa Clause,
   don't let that deter you
from giving to Billy
   any gift that you want to."

"For, you see, Billy will never
turn someone away
when his help is needed
any time of the day."

Jolly Old St. Nick
was just about done.
He couldn't think when
he'd had so much fun.

Maybe the list would
go missing next year
and more tales of his kids
from the teachers he'd hear.

Mr. Cox, the last teacher
    to give a report,
looked like Santa himself,
    was the round, jolly sort.

He said that the children
    in their little town
were the best—very best
    that could ever be found.

GRADE
REPORT

He chortled with Santa
and tried to recall
an occasion where someone
was sent to the hall.

And then he remembered
a few months ago
the problem he'd had
with his sweet little Flo.

He was teaching the kids
about sharp notes and flat,
when down on a big
whoopee cushion he sat!

The children were howling
when Mr. Cox said,
"I expect a confession,
or I shall see red."

Little Flo pleaded guilty
to the terrible crime
by raising her hand
in the quick nick of time.

"So, Santa, she's honest.
I don't blame her a bit;
to stop collapsing from laughter
was the hardest thing yet!"

When Santa had finished
delivering the toys,
he knew not to worry
about his girls and boys.

They were all being taught
by teachers who care,
good people he found
in the schools everywhere.

Their skill and their wisdom
helped him save the day.
Now Christmas was here,
he could go on his way.

Then he called as his reindeer
flew up with no fuss,
"Merry Christmas, dear teachers,
you all get an A+."

Merry Christmas